I0571647

OUR STORM

JANICKA SHULER

INTRODUCTION

My name is Darnice. I have four amazing children: Janay, who at the time of this story was thirteen; Pooter, who was eleven; James, who was six; and Messiah, who was two.

This is our storm.

Saturday, October 8, 2017

I was hospitalized due to some upper respiratory issues. I couldn't physically see my children, but I spoke to them every day. Lamar, my boyfriend, had been a blessing. He was managing to be by my side night and day while taking care of our children and household.

My two younger sons' grandmother had called to check on me to see if I needed anything or if I needed my two youngest boys' father to get them while I was in the hospital to help take the load off Lamar. I told her yes.

Wednesday, October 11, 2017

When my boys left with their father. I had no idea that I wouldn't talk to them or see them again for two months. Earlier that day, I was missing my Messiah so much I couldn't take it. Lamar said, "Do you want me to bring James and Messiah?"

I said yes. When I saw Messiah, I noticed he had a scar on his forehead. I said, "Lamar where did you get this scar from?"

I said yes. When I saw Messiah, I noticed he had a scar on his forehead. I said, "Lamar where did he get this scar from?"

Lamar said that Messiah and Pooter had been playing on the steps, and Messiah fell down the steps. Pooter had taken the carpet from the upstairs hallway steps and dining area during the summer, so there were lots of nails. Everyone in the house either stepped on them or may have gotten a scratch or cut.

2

Our nightmare began after Lamar got Janay and James off to school. He came to the hospital and was there by my side, as he did every day. At about 11:30 or 11:45 in the morning, I got a call from my niece's mother, who lived with me. She said two Children Services workers and a deputy sheriff had come to my house trying to pry their way inside, yelling, "Where is Darnice Johnson? Where are James and Messiah and Pooter?" and claiming that the kids were being abused.

She was yelling back at them, "Darnice is in the hospital. I'm not telling y'all nothing. I don't have nothing to say to y'all. If y'all want to know anything, call Darnice."

So, of course, they did just that. The trio knocks on my hospital door and came right in. At this point, Lamar had left because he had an appointment. But right after my niece's mom called and warned me, I called Janay at school. She said, "Mom, I haven't talked to or told nobody we get beat. We don't get beat, Mom."

I said, "okay, let me call Pooter." I tried for about half an hour to call my son's school, which was Mahoning County High. They refused to put my son on the phone and hung up on me continuously.

Then the trio came into my room, yelling. The deputy sheriff yelled, "your son told us your boyfriend has been beating him."

The whole time, one of the Children Services workers had a cell phone flipping through pictures of old dried-up scars.

Then the sheriff said, "and your son has a scar on his face."

I'll remind you, I had been hospitalized, so I hadn't seen my son. I called my niece's mom and said, "these people are talking about Pooter getting a scratch on his face."

She said, "no, Darnice. A few days ago, Pooter and Messiah was playing together on the steps and they both fell down."

I had her on speakerphone the entire time, so the trio could hear the same story Lamar had told me earlier.

So I said, "okay, did y'all hear that?"

Then the deputy started yelling, "no. Where's Lamar at? I want to talk to him. Your son said he has been beating on him."

I was yelling, "get the fuck out! My son ain't told y'all that. Bye-bye. Get out. Get out."

The Children Services lady said, "ma'am, you need to listen. Lamar needs to leave the home."

I continued yelling, "get the fuck out! My son ain't told y'all no shit like that."

The deputy sheriff yelled, "oh, you don't wanna listen? You don't want to cooperate?" I said, "bye."

About half an hour later, here comes Children Services calling me saying they have custody of my two oldest. Since the younger two weren't at home during the incident, they couldn't obtain custody of them. They were still with their dad, which turned out to be a mistake on my part.

I started yelling and cursing, and then I hung up the phone. I immediately called Janay's cell. At this point, the sheriff had already picked her up from school. She was attending William Holmes McGuffey. Pooter was already in the car, she said, and she also told me that her school had transferred her records to Mahoning County High School, which made no sense to me or my daughter.

"You're not going there," I told her. "Nobody called me to notify me of any of that information. I'll handle that later. What happened? Why did that sheriff pick y'all up?"

She said, "mommy, I don't know what's going on. I got called down to the office, and he said I had to go with him."

I said to myself, *them dirty muthafuckas. Against my better judgment, I fell for their bullshit.* All BS. Then I told Janay, "yeah, because Pooter went to school telling them Lamar beats him. I'ma beat his lying ass."

Janay started yelling, "Pooter, why you tell them that? You know we don't get beat at all."

Still so very confused, not even knowing what was really going on while they were driving with the sheriff, Janay told me, "Pooter keeps saying, 'where we going? You taking us home? We going to my mom's house. I want to go home.' The sheriff says, 'yeah, I'm taking y'all home.'" She added, "mommy, I just looked at Pooter and shook my head. I knew we wasn't going home, but Pooter was still believing the man."

It was about three thirty or four o'clock. And now this Children Services worker was asking me if there was anyone who could take my children. I had two sisters, but they lived in Cleveland. I called my brother, who lived closest to me, and of course he flew down to the Children Services office. But they did a criminal background check.

At this point, I was still angry, mainly at Pooter for telling these lies. Janay's cell phone started going to voicemail. The rest of that evening and into the night, I was a nervous wreck, thinking, *where are my kids*?

Later that evening, I got released from the hospital, and I was crying, asking Lamar, "where are my kids? Where are my kids?" I said, "keep calling Janay's cell. It keeps going to voicemail, and I don't know where they're at!"

Thursday, October 12, 2017

I called the agency at eight thirty sharp, inquiring about my children. Of course, my luck, they gave me the intake worker from hell, so she was like, "yes, we took custody of you children Janay and Pooter. Also, where are James and Messiah?"

I said, "why? They don't live with me. They live with their dad. They don't have nothing to do with this situation." My children really lived with me, but out of fear they'd say they're taking custody of them too, that's what I told her.

She said, "well, we just want to make sure they're safe."

I responded, "I told you, they don't live here." She asked me, when was the last time I had seen them? I said, "it's been a while."

Janay had seen right through them, because they had already asked her as well and she told them, "my brothers live with their dad." She wasn't stupid and wasn't going to give up any information, especially to anybody she felt was a threat to our family. We didn't want the boys involved in this mess. Janay didn't know how happy I was to find out she had given the intake worker this information, but that's Janay – she's always been very intelligent.

So this intake worker starts to go on and on about how Pooter told her Lamar was beating him. Now, the crazy thing is, I have four children altogether, and just Pooter was getting beat on? Yeah, okay. So she starts saying Lamar could have child abuse charges brought against him and how it's unsafe for my kids to come back home, and could I think of anyone to take my children.

I was so angry, hurt, and mad at Pooter, so I said, "that little liar can stay there, but I'll find someone for Janay."

I called my cousin and explained to her what was going on. She agreed to take Janay, so arrangements were made. Things got set up with Children Services for my cousin to come in and take fingerprints and a background check.

Later on, I got a call, and it was Janay. She immediately broke down crying, saying, "Mommy, I want to come home! I want to come home!"

I started crying too. I said, "baby, you're going to come home. Stop crying." I said, "are you okay? Where is your cell phone?"

She said, "mommy, it went dead. But they took it. They said we're not allowed to have cell phones."

I asked her, "Where's that money I told you to hold for me when I was in the hospital?"

She said, "they took that too. They said they'd put it up for me."

Janay said that as soon as she and Pooter arrived, staff asked, "aren't y'all the children who get beat?"

She said she and Pooter looked at each other and said, "what? We don't get beat."

I said, "everything is going to be okay. You're going to your cousin's house."

She said, "what about Pooter?"

I said, "that little liar can stay there."

I spoke again with the intake worker, and she stated I was having an adjudication hearing the next day at ten o'clock at the JJC. I kept telling myself Pooter was a big liar, and everybody would see. Anybody who knew me and Lamar already knew we weren't beating our children.

Friday, October 13, 2017

I went to the adjudication meeting, which was for Children Services to tell the judge they had to take immediate action because my children were unsafe at home – because Pooter was getting beat and I was being uncooperative. All this because I yelled and cursed them out and made them leave my hospital room because I didn't want to hear the lies they were telling.

Janay repeatedly told every person who questioned her that she and her siblings did not get beat. Janay was so upset and angry at Pooter. My brother and sisters were as well. Janay was turning fourteen on October 17, and of course, now her birthday plans were ruined.

After the adjudication hearing, I went to Daybreak to get the money I gave Janay. She saw me, ran, and jumped on me, yelling, "mommy! Mommy, I missed you!" I squeezed her tight and told her I loved and missed her too. I saw Pooter but continued to ignore him, not even making eye contact.

I know now that I was wrong. I should have known better than that my son would betray me like that. The devil was working on me hard – me and my children. Something serious was going on. It was about to get deep.

I told Janay my cousin was coming to get her later on that afternoon, and that I'd see and talk to her then. My sister Mesha came into town from Cleveland, and she picked up Janay from my cousin's house and brought her home to do her hair. Janay went back Friday night.

Saturday, October 14, 2017

It was about six thirty in the morning. I walked into the house, just getting off of work; I worked ten at night until six in the morning. I went into my room and started praying. Lamar had been letting this stress him out to the core. He didn't say it, but I saw the look on his face. I also noticed a change in the way he was acting. I told Lamar, "baby, we are going to get through this because we're a family, and that's what families do. Now, Lamar, take my hand and let's pray."

We prayed silently, and then he said, "now is the time I'm going to have to put my faith to the test."

"Yes, babe," I agreed. Then I got up. I mean, I don't know what got into me, but I started yelling – yelling at the top of my lungs. I had never yelled that loud in my life. I mean, it was to the point where I had a sore throat for five days after. I couldn't eat and could only drink water. Anything else that I tried to consume burned my throat.

I yelled and cried and paced the room. I kept asking Lamar, "are you listening to me?"

He said, "I'm listening, babe. Let it out. Let it out."

I yelled from about 6:45 a.m. until 9:47 a.m. At that point, I had lost it. I had lost my cool. I mean, I broke down. The crazy thing is, I didn't see this coming.

Lamar said, "babe, I knew you were going to break."

I said, "how? I don't break easily. I just don't."

Lamar said, "babe, because it was about your kids."

I said, "Lamar, breaking ain't me. I don't break. I've been broken down twice in life. Well, this just now makes the third."

Sunday, October 15, 2017

I worked Saturday night into early Sunday morning. My son Pooter was rushed to Akron, Ohio, because he was trying to jump out of a two-story house. They said he was so out of control, he had to be shot with a tranquilizer.

This is not my son. He has behavior problems, but not like this. Janay said, "mom, from the time we got to Daybreak, Pooter kept asking the staff, 'can I call my mom? Can I call my mom?'" She said, "mommy, Pooter is being bad, really bad, misbehaving and cursing. He ran away almost every day."

My baby boy was going through it, and all alone – all because he wanted me, his mommy, and didn't understand why I had given up on him all of sudden, why I felt the need to not want him anymore or why I wouldn't even talk to him.

Monday, October 16, 2017

I sent Janay a text message saying *I love you James & Messiah to death but if y'all ever betray me like Pooter did I'll turn my back on y'all too.*

She said, "mommy, I miss Pooter. I love my brother. He's the closet thing I got to my dad. When am I going to see Pooter again?" She added, "ma, them people tricked Pooter. He didn't tell them he was getting beat. He said he gets whoopings. That's it."

Several school staff and a deputy had surrounded my son when he came to school on October 11, early that morning, intimidating him with badgering questions and putting words in his mouth that he never said. I cried, because for five days, I had denied my son and disowned him. I had literally wanted nothing to do with him, because I was listening to these devilish people.

I hurried and called someone who has known Pooter since he was baby. She knew what was going on because I had already called and informed her. I said, "they tricked my baby." I said, "please, please get my son out of Daybreak immediately."

So when he returned from Akron Children's Hospital, she went down to the Children Services agency and got her background check and fingerprints done. Later on that afternoon, my baby was out of Daybreak thanks to someone I considered family. I made sure I told Pooter I loved him and I was so sorry.

I cried. I mean, I was so hurt that I had believed my son betrayed me. My heart was broken, and my soul was on fire because my children could not come home. It hurt me so bad, but I felt a little ease knowing they were with family.

James and Messiah were with their dad. The two of us had a coparenting relationship. We were cool and on the same page when it came to our sons – or so I thought. He was like, "yeah, I got you. Whatever you need me to do."

I said, "well, call the intake worker. Let her know you have custody of the boys, because I don't want her trying to take them from me too." He said, "okay, I'll give her a call."

I then again told my son, "Pooter, I want you to know that you did nothing wrong, and I'm not mad because you said you get whoopings, because anyone who knows us knows y'all don't get beat. But anybody who tries to tear a family apart for no reason ain't nothing but pure white devils."

I say *white devils* because the people who were making our lives a living hell were white people. I am not a racist; if they were black, yellow, or red, I would have said black, yellow, or red devils. The devil will come in disguise in any shape, color, or form, and what they were doing to my family was devilish.

I mean, this was a mess. All this had taken place in less than a week of Children Services removing my children from our home. This was truly a nightmare that I wouldn't wish on anyone. My children and I had never experienced anything like this before.

Tuesday, October 17, 2017

Pooter's school at the time, Mahoning County High, called me on speakerphone saying that they had him in the office and he wanted to speak with me. Now, they never stated I was on speaker, but I already knew. I could tell.

Pooter said, "hi, mom."

I said, "hey, Poo. What are you doing?"

He said, "nothing. I'm at school."

I said, "okay."

He said, "mommy, I'm going to daycare after school." It was the one he had been at, but not currently. We'd known them for a long time.

I believe my son was a victim that day. He got called down to the office and got ambushed. He was alone and scared.

Now, this was nothing new. When Pooter got angry, he would tear up an office, classroom, or whatever he felt necessary at the moment – throwing objects, chairs, and whatever he felt at the time. The school had called me a few times mainly to calm him down and get him under control, because they couldn't.

I was furious with everybody involved, so I told my son that the next time he tore that school up, they better not call me, because I didn't care anymore what he did. I said anybody who makes our life hell for no reason is just a devil, and all them up there ain't nothing but some white devils.

He said, "ma, they laughing at you, and they got you on speakerphone."

I said, "I know, and I don't care. I want them to hear me."

A staff member then said, "bye-bye, Ms. Johnson," and disconnected the call.

As soon as he got off the phone with me, my son began tearing that school apart. So the school called the intake worker at Children

Services, who then decided to hospitalize Pooter at Belmont Pines, like he was some mental patient.

Wednesday, October 18, 2017

Pooter went to Belmont Pines on October 18 and was there for almost a week. I called the intake worker, and I begged and pleaded with her to allow me to speak with my son. She said no.

I said, "he's not crazy – this is *making* him crazy. All he wants is his mom." I said, "Pooter is a mama's boy."

She said, "you can't talk to him. He's in the hospital."

I said to the intake worker, "can't you see? My son just wants his mom. That's all he wants. Y'all are making him crazy." And I was about there with him. I was the only person he wanted and needed, and these white devils were telling him, *No, you can't talk to or see your mother*, with no explanation why. My baby needed me so bad, and I needed him too. All I wanted to do was talk to my baby and give him my love and reassurance. I was damn near like a walking zombie.

So I did what I knew best: I prayed. I mean, I prayed hard, too, from being stressed out daily and crying from everything that had been taking place in our lives. I mean, I had a child who was having a mental breakdown, all because he wanted me, his mother, and neither one of us could do anything about it.

My baby began to carry a pain bigger than him. We needed each other. I started asking myself, *Why? What did I do? Did I do too much of this or not enough of that*? I said to myself, *why are we going through this*? I mean, it was one thing after another.

Pooter had been playing for the Youngstown Titans since he was five. All the while he was in Belmont Pines, he kept asking his guardian to have me call his coach and tell the coach not to give his position away. He loves football; it was the only thing he was good at.

Of course, I relayed the message. The next week, his team won the playoff game.

Saturday, October 28, 2017

Pooter was able to play in the championship game a week later. It was the first time I had seen Pooter since October 7. Just to finally be able to hug and kiss my son was a great feeling. I gave him a big hug, because after the game, he had to be released to his guardian, not me – but the guardian was of my choice and one of Pooter's favorite people in the world.

Monday, October 30, 2017

A family visit was supposed to take place, because Pooter was about to go live in Cleveland with my sister until further notice. None of the kids were in the home, but Pooter was the only one leaving Youngstown. All he wanted was to see me, his brothers, and his sister. My initial caseworker had set the visit up at Pooter's request.

The visit went on as planned – but without my two youngest boys. I just cried. My family was split up. I hadn't seen or talked to my boys since October 10, the day Lamar brought them to the hospital to see me. It was the same night their father had come to pick them up.

Janay and I went to a Halloween party that was hosted by my younger boys' aunt. Their father pushed me and yelled, "why are you here?" The kids weren't allowed to see me, talk to me, or be around me; if they were caught with any type of contact with me, that caseworker would take the boys from him.

Funny thing: up until that day, my boys' dad called me, texted me, checked in on me, gave me rides to work – I mean, we had no issue with each other, or at least, so I thought. But because his girlfriend was there, he decided to put on a show, and so did she. She even had the nerve to say to me, "that's why you ain't got yo kids." Now, just because it came from her mouth, all I could do was laugh. It was funny to me.

Instead of complying with my caseworker, returning calls, or anything pertaining to my boys, he had side dealings with the intake worker from hell, who had nothing to do with the case anymore. But the devil was working without anyone knowing what was going on. She, the white devil intake worker, told my kids' father not to speak with anyone but her. I was still not allowed to have contact with my boys.

I just prayed, because prayer changes things. My boys' dad kept my children from me for two months. I'm like, how could this be happening? You came to pick them up for a few days from our house, I felt like I was carrying the weight of a mountain.

I kept saying, *come on, white devil, what's next? What have you got for me?* I couldn't have my children, all four of them. I told myself I wanted to die. It was nightmare after nightmare. I wanted to quit and give up on everything, because the only thing that mattered to me had been taken from me – my children, my life. They completed me. Without them, I was nothing.

As I yelled, *come on, white devil, what's next?* I found that the devil had plenty more in store for me. I was so worried and stressed out because I hadn't seen or spoken with my younger two. Sleep was the only time I had peace, because this living daydream didn't visit me at night. Sleep became an instinct, because I kept enduring so much pain, and it was so unbearable.

I mean, I prayed so much all through the day. I said, "Lamar, all my life I have never had patience until now – the patience of waiting to get my children back home." It was out of my control, but every day I spoke with Janay and Pooter. Pooter got settled in okay in Cleveland with my sister. He started his new school and was doing good.

The intake worker had said there would be a case plan designed for me to complete in order to get my children back. I was still at a loss as to what was taking place. None of my children had said they were being abused, not even Pooter. I got so frustrated. More and more was put on my plate, and each time I began to sink, it got heavier. There was no ending, no resolution, and worst of all, no kids.

But I tell you what: as soon as she told me to do something, I started right away. I had no car, but my children were on the line, so there was nothing that would stop me. My methods of transportation were the WRTA, a taxi, or my feet. Nothing stopped me – nothing.

Tuesday, November 14, 2017

Anger-management and parenting classes were the first things I was told to begin, so I did. I wanted these people out of my life. Lamar and I walked out the door together for my first class; he was going with me. He was by my side every step of the way. He even agreed to be put on the case plan, and he didn't have to be.

But as we stepped outside on the porch, the US marshals came swarming up, yelling, "is your name Darnice Johnson?" I said yes, and they said, "turn around, you're under arrest. You've been charged with a felony 3 inciting a riot."

A month before, when I was on the phone with Pooter and he tore the school up, they allegedly said I told him to do it. So because he tore it up, I got charged with this violent crime. The very next day, my brother bonded me out. So now I was arrested, with my face all over the internet. I even made front cover of the newspaper. I was getting hit front to back and side to side.

I said it again: *come on, white devils. What's next*? My faith was so strong that even waking up in jail, I still prayed. I say my faith was stronger than my strength, because God says he'll never put more on you than you can handle. For a split second, I was hanging from a loose piece of thin thread, because at this point I'm fighting to get my kids back plus a criminal case. You just don't know how many times I wanted to give up. But God says he gives battles to his strong soldiers, and I had no options. I was determined to get my children back and restore my family.

Life was wearing and tearing me down, but Satan was getting angry, because every time he threw something at me, it didn't stick. My kids just don't know how strong I was. At some points, I surprised my damn self.

Even though I had a strong support system, mentally and physically, I was not all there. I was gone in a way. It was like I had become so alone that in a room full of people, I saw no one.

Now Janay, who was still with my older cousin, began to have issues, so I asked my brother's girlfriend if Janay could stay with her. She agreed. I was grateful.

So now the holidays were approaching, and still nothing from my younger boys. My two-year-old, Messiah, couldn't talk yet, so I could not rest. I kept thinking, *is he going to think I just abandoned him*? Thanksgiving came, and me and my siblings were all together, along with my nieces and nephews and Janay and Pooter.

Monday, December 4, 2017

At the second adjudication date at JJC regarding my case, there was a happy outcome. Love finally came back to me that I hadn't felt since my kids were taken from me. Three out of my four were now back home – Janay, James, and Messiah. All my prayers, all my worries, had come to an end regarding my two younger boys, because they were back home and safe.

I had to have Campbell police escort me to get my children; their father was trying his best to keep them from me in every way possible. He was waving some paper around, thinking he had custody. Well, the paper was only to verify that he was able to take them to doctor appointments and things of that nature. I waited a damn hour for him to release my children to me – my babies, James and Messiah.

Funny thing is, he hadn't seen or called the boys for two months prior to getting them on October 10, and that was his choice, not mine. Then, instead of working with me about our children, he was working against me. I would have never done anything like that to him. I now look at my boys' dad so differently. He has been forgiven, though. Baby James said he asked Dad to call me. His dad said he didn't know my number. James said he told his dad, "I want my mommy," and his dad's girlfriend said, "she in jail."

I said, "it's okay, son. I'm here now. I won't leave you now."

Thursday, December 14, 2017

I was indicted by a grand jury, and the incident was on the news. I lost my job that day, but by the grace of God, two weeks later, I was hired somewhere else. Now, finally, all my children are together again. Even though Pooter was still with Sandra, we spent weekends and holidays together. I finished anger-management and parenting classes upon getting James and Janay enrolled in school. It took me about a month.

Monday, January 8, 2018

I attended my last adjudication hearing. But Pooter still had to remain with Sandra, and I still had to get a psychiatric eval, which was my last assignment on my care plan.

They wanted to come to my house three days a week. This was something that had just been added. Then Children Services decided to send certified mail to my home, which was a child-support hearing scheduled for March 8, 2018. So here came more crying. I just wanted this to be over. Now, out of the four children, I had three in my home. So why wasn't my fourth one home? This was a horrific time, but I never quit praying, as we should every day, through bad and good times.

I decided to write about it. Writing had become so therapeutic to me. I mean, it was such a good feeling. It also helped save me. It helped save my soul. These were some very trying times, and it definitely became a testimony that deserved to be heard. Christ had made a difference in my life, which made our story worth telling.

Because I had put all my faith in God and trusted him with my life – I mean, I put *everything* that we were going through literally in his hands – I consistently said my faith became bigger than my strength, because it was God who carried me through. I was weak; I had no more fight in me. This was a battle that had me feeling like a walking zombie. I had a broken heart and a soul that was on fire. When I finally could get sleep, I was afraid to. I was scared the devil had more attacks to fire at me. When I did find sleep, he went there too. I began to have anxiety attacks.

As humans, we make mistakes. We were made imperfect. As a mother, I'm going to make mistakes when it comes to my children. There is no such thing as a perfect parent. It's unheard of. But we learn as we grow.

I can admit my wrongs, and as angry as I was at those white devils for turning my family upside down, in a moment of weakness, I should never have told my son that if he got mad again to tear the MF school up. I told him, "I don't care if you do, son, especially when it's people trying to tear our family apart. When people are trying to give our family hell, you give them hell back, and they better not call me, because I don't give a fuck."

The actions that followed only added more trauma and hurt to our family. I should have known that Pooter was ready to bring hurt or grief to whoever he thought was trying to separate our family, because he wanted to be home. With him being so emotional, at this point, everything he was feeling, he made those white devils feel. He broke windows. He tried to fight the security guard and every staff member within arm's reach. He was completely uncontrollable. No one could stop him. He really tore that school up.

My kids had never been in a situation like this before. They were in three different places when they should have been at home. I love my children, and they love me. Everything I do is for them.

Pooter has always been a mama's boy, so this was not setting in easy with him. To tell a child he can't come home with his mother, the only person that he has, and to tell me I can't talk to my children, who are the only beings that matter to me in this world – the separation was just pure heart damage for me. I experienced every emotion known to man. I was crying, stressed, depressed, suicidal, and heartbroken. My soul was on fire with anxiety, anger, irritation, and betrayal. My unwillingness to fight an unwanted battle was ludicrous to me. I never understood why I had to fight Children Services, a school, a criminal case, and even my youngest boys' father.

That was the last thing I ever expected. He should have been working with me instead of against me. All these years later, after two children together, it was like I didn't even know this man. He became a stranger to me. I realized that my reality was that I had laid down with a stranger. He definitely opened up my blind eyes.

I forgave him, but I didn't forget anything. Someone like that doesn't mean my children, his children, our children any good. He definitely doesn't deserve to be in our life. I know without a doubt he'd never physically hurt my children. He knows I'm not perfect, but I'm a great parent when it comes to our boys – hell, all my children. I've lost so much respect for him as a man. I mean, even though we weren't together and had our share of troubles in the past, the only thing that mattered to me was our children. We had a cordial relationship, and in the blink of an eye, he folded on me. So for that, I told myself, he forever ended anything and everything with me.

My ultimate goal in life is to go above and beyond for my children's sake. They deserve so much. My goal also is to never look back and dwell or let this situation detour or determine my future life ventures. I'm a fighter, and this is an example of the saying, "nothing worth having or fighting for comes easy."

Lamar was amazing. He stood by my side the whole time. He said, "I'm trying to keep you sane." With the kids being gone, he was the only thing I had to look forward to coming home. I had never before felt this empty and alone. Lamar let me know I wasn't alone; he was there with me, and we were going to get through this together.

I told him how I loved and appreciated him being there for me the way he had. Because he was there with me and had to experience the multiple situations that occurred, he also dealt with a lot of my rantings, which I know was difficult for him because he didn't deserve any of it coming from me. But he was patient with me. I am grateful for him. I never had a man put up with me as long as he did or take care of me the way he did, especially when I was sick.

I was told that sometimes God will tear down a family to rebuild, and that's exactly what He did. One thing I realized that God would do in a situation like this is open your blind eyes, because He wants your undivided attention. When all else failed, this was His way of getting my attention, of telling me He was right there and wanted me to become closer to Him.

I remember when I got the younger boys back, Pooter said, "ma, why did the boys come back home? Because I prayed?"

I said, "I prayed too, Poo. I want you to continue to pray every day."

This situation brought more prayer into my life than ever. My eleven year-old prays more and loves to go to church. His heart is humongous. He has a great head on his shoulders. He is a kid, so of course he'll make mistakes in his life.

As time went by, I learned and was taught a few things. As I said, I never had patience before. Well, God gave patience to me. He also was trying to tell me that the schools my children were attending were not meant for them, because he had something better in mind.

I have dealt with losing my mother at the age of nine and my father at the age of eighteen. My first love (my two oldest children's father, whom I met at the age of thirteen) was murdered in 2012. I lost a child in 2013 and my grandmother Johnson that same year. Both of my grandmothers were special to me. They were my go-to in my time of need, my reassurance.

My father's mother – my grandma Johnson – was full of the Holy Spirit. Besides praying in any situation, without me even telling her something was bothering me, her soul quietly knew and calmed me down. Whatever uncomfortable feeling was felt within me was taken away.

She was my Mama, my mother's mother, who got custody of me and my siblings when my mother died. Mama, the life of the party, got sick and passed away September 19, 2016. I could literally write a book about her. She was my mother's mother. I'm the oldest grandchild. Mama was heaven-sent. I thank God for allowing her to be my Mama. God, I thank you for your gracious act of love, for lending her to me.

Even losing so many people who meant so much to me didn't compare to the emptiness I felt in this horrific experience with my children. One thing I try not to do now is judge. Even though I had good people on my side, all the love was still not enough. Lamar, who was there with me physically, got the short end of the stick. These were my children, my world, my life, the only thing that mattered to me. I had to fight alone. It was me, Darnice Johnson, who had to fight all these cases. So this is why I said I felt so alone during these trying times.

I remember Lamar kept saying, "I guess now is when I start testing my faith." And that's exactly what we did upon speaking everything into existence. As you can see, our faith was tested in every way possible. What is faith? The Bible says it's the substance of things hoped for and the evidence of things not seen. Wow, just writing this puts me in awe. Glory be to God.

Our faith was tested so that we could know God's faithfulness. You have to know God is amazing. I mean, to believe in someone you can't see and to know when you call on him that he's right there by your side. Countless times, when you put your trust in God, it becomes your faith. It becomes your reasoning to believe he will carry you through whatever you're going through. I now tell myself I have faith in God, and because I do, I don't need anything else. My faith in the Lord got me through this. God is amazing.

I didn't write this story for sympathy. I just wanted people to know, don't ever think that you're exempt from anything. Even the most faithful man known to God can experience trials and tribulation. We often don't see the devil's work, even when there are signs. We may just ignore those signs.

That was me. I ignored all the signs, which actually started with my children being enrolled at Mahoning County High School. That's when the devil's work began. I swear, life will take you through things you wouldn't imagine. I kept telling Lamar, "this is an obstacle, but we will get through this, because we are a family and that's what families do." I definitely called it an obstacle, because I knew this was going to be a hard situation, especially when you got people making it that way from the beginning.

I know that for every bad situation you have, the Lord will walk you through. He also will give you glory days. Here at the age of thirty-one, I have four children, and together we have faced unwanted life experiences. Since the age of nine when I lost my mother, on April 15, 1996, I have always felt alone inside. I'll probably feel this way for a lifetime. But I'm rock solid and not easily broken.

So throughout this crazy case, Pooter, who didn't like to listen, had been giving my sister he was living with a hard time. I tried a different approach with him. I texted him every morning telling him I loved him and asking him to behave. I prayed for my son, as I did for all my children.

Thursday, February 15, 2018

Oh, and the child support hearing – I didn't go. So of course, they sent me a letter to pay child support. With my criminal case still going, I had that hearing on February 15, with a court-appointed lawyer. The only deal the prosecutor was willing to give was for me to plead guilty to a felony 3, be on adult parole for three years, and do jail time. I asked this duck of a lawyer how much jail time, and he said he didn't know; it was up to the judge.

I said, "no, I'm not taking that deal, and I don't want you as my lawyer either. I'm getting a paid lawyer, somebody who's going to fight for me, because you're working for them, not for me."

Now I have no felonies at all. This man as my lawyer must've taken me for a fool. I contacted a criminal defense lawyer and paid out of pocket. I was being railroaded, but I wasn't going for it. I was a single mother who financially took care of four children, and going to jail was not an option.

About a month later, I received notice for another pretrial hearing. It was after I told this court-appointed lawyer I didn't want him representing me. His secretary calls me and says the hearing got canceled because the lawyer was busy doing another case, and they would be sending out another letter.

OUR STORM

1

We serve such an amazing God. I sit back in such awe. I am honoring and thanking God for everything he has done for my family and for me.

Pain brought me the love of my life. Pain brought me the ability to endure hurt. I learned about finding strength, faith, patience, humility, focus, love, and compassion. Much more pain brought upon me the reassurance that God loved me so much, even under the testing of my stormy trials.

It was then, when I was about to give up because I could not bear any more pain from the great loss I had experienced, that he gave me love. When I thought I had lost love, he added it. The pain was temporary, but God's love is forever.

I'm living proof of how the God we serve is unbelievably, undeniably merciful. He uses broken people like me to teach somebody, to touch somebody, to strengthen others' belief in God. And just as he did it for me, I assure you he'll do it for you.

When I feel pain, I know God has more blessings to add to my life. I say that with strong confidence. Not seeing him or not knowing what his acts are, my confidence remains the same. The only thing that's different is the amount of faith I have. Each time it increases, it has to in order for me to grow closer to Christ.

Writing is how I let my pain out. God has a purpose for our pain. Look at how he has used me as a living testament.

I fell in love with writing. When I would begin writing, I never wanted to stop. When you're on the road to greatness, you're going to at least suffer some kind of trial.

In your lifetime, suffering from trials only builds strength and endurance. It's not the suffering itself, it's how you handle it that brings the proper outcome. I am now able to believe and trust in God wholeheartedly. He has something better for me while I'm in pain.

If it wasn't for my trials, I wouldn't have been able to allow God to work his merciful ways in my life. God is actually working at his best in our lives when we face trying times. Then he uses someone like me to tell the miraculous and glorified ways he acted in my life.

My life changed the moment I began writing. I was able to write for eight or more hours straight because I loved it so much. As I was writing, it almost felt as if the pain didn't exist. I only began to feel it again when I took a rest from writing. It hurt more to stop my body. I just wanted to keep going.

I have never been that focused and passionate about anything in my entire life – not this way, anyway. I was so passionate, and it was the first time I felt that fire and desire. I came to writing quickly. It was like running blindfolded. It seemed like I had done it for many years, or my entire life.

It started to become easier – almost like the light feather pen I was gently holding was doing all work. I focused more on what I loved. Even the pain wasn't going to stop me. I didn't even realize this. The whole time I just was returning the energy I was feeling. The greater the pain I felt, the greater my writing became.

My family, our family, was chosen for God's greater good. My children were born with the greatness like me. Once the ignition is set, God is going to work his miraculous and astonishing ways in their lives.

My children have special capabilities. You will not believe what you are watching. But that's what God does. He works in unbelievable, unthinkable, and unimaginable ways. The legacy I'm creating with my offspring is going to be so amazing. My children are going to be able to touch and achieve the highest of levels, because the way I'm teaching them is that the higher you become, the more humble you become. I'm teaching them to become more selfless, loving, compassionate, generous, and kindhearted in the eyes of the world.

They're climbing ladders in the eyes of God. They're also stepping down. My kids understand that they're able to fulfill their dreams and do what they love because of God's favor, grace, and love. There's nothing we can ever do to deserve this, so in return, you are to show God gratitude. We are only blessed to become a blessing. My children are going to bless with love in their hearts, and they're going to love doing it.

Our storm was meant to be. It was created for a reason. How can someone experience the loss of a house if they never had one?

What a great feeling of pain when you have your family one day and the next they're gone. The losses we have to deal with seem so inhumane. To enable your Christlike image, you have to become humble. That is why my children are the way they are. It started early in their lives so each feature can grow into maturity.

I believe my children's reward for their faithfulness amongst many is found in Jeremiah 29:11: "'For I know the plans I have for you,' declares the Lord, 'plans to prosper you and not to harm you, plans to give you hope and a future.'" There was nothing I could've done differently. Our lives were planned before we were born.

In fact, this trial taught my children a great lesson. Instead of creating hearts that were tough and full of anger, it softened their hearts, allowing them to become humble and weak. So that God can live out his plans entirely, my children have found peace at home. In fact, home is where their hearts are. Home is where our horror story began, but it's also where it ended.

3

That intake worker's personal hatred for me was so strong that she could be careless of who else was suffering. I was the one person she came at full throttle with the intent of my destruction. Stupid dummy never thought for a blink of an eye that she was taking down four children too, in ways unimaginable and unthinkable. You have to ask yourself, *how can a person who has nothing but evil intent from the first day until your last encounter want the best for your children?*

Every last thing she did to me became personal and was meant to hit as hard as possible. She wanted to take me down, but she didn't. If her intentions were good from the start, she probably would have kept her sanity, because she damn near lost it trying to take mine from me.

This intake worker from hell called the Social Security office and notified them that her agency had custody of Pooter. Social Security stopped his benefits and sent me a letter stating I owed them from whatever date the intake worker gave them up until her notifying them. At the child support hearing, I owed like $1,500 in back child support, because she was the one who initiated for me to pay child support.

She called the Department of Jobs and Family Services, again stating that her agency had custody of Pooter, but in doing so – all out of spite, I'll remind you – he gave *Janay,* my daughter's name, instead of Pooter's, which is *Jondell.* End result was Janay's medical insurance was stopped. If her intentions were good from the start, she would never have made that mistake. She was doing everything in a hurry to hurt me in as many ways as possible.

I was still receiving Pooter's SSI check even though he wasn't in the home for his benefit, not mine. Whether he lived with me or not, I was still his mother, and I didn't want to put any financial burden on my

25

sister. I mean, she already let him stay with her, but as his parent, the full responsibility was still on me to take care of him. That's my child, and nothing was going to stop me from taking care of him no matter what.

Once his check was cut off, nobody received it, and the child services agency did nothing for him. I believe they paid my sister's rent one month and gave her a food voucher about two times. This whole situation came about because I was trying to make sure my sister could get anything she could, since the intake worker was so malicious. She had it in for me from the first day we met.

They did nothing for my son, but I didn't care. I still took care of my baby, so I'll never complain about it. I only was angered by this woman and her devilish ways. She was so hard up on hurting me in whichever way she could. My child was never her concern; she couldn't care less about his well-being. She had vengeance set for me, and nothing was stopping her.

4

I felt all the pain from everything that was done to me. But God will let evil go on only but so long. He's for love, not hateful wicked intentions. That's why nothing that evil intake worker tried lasted.

My caseworker even told me that when my two little ones came home, the intake worker wasn't happy about it at all. Initially, they were with their dad, and he and the intake worker paired up against me and wholeheartedly tried to keep my boys away from me. For two months, they succeeded.

The hurtful part about it is, she took my kids from me, saying no contact at all, like they were being harmed – just to have them with their dad, where my boys suffered verbal abuse and physical abuse from their father's girlfriend, who puts on a major front like she cares at all about my babies. She tolerates them, that's all. Even the word *tolerate* is stretching the truth on how she feels about them.

She took two years of love from him after being there for only two months. His happy full smiling energetic soul was gone. My baby looked at me as if I were a stranger. He was an emotionless zombie. God saved my baby's soul and heart just in time.

Baby James told me different things the girlfriend said and did. He said, "I don't like her because when we had to live with Daddy, she was mean to Messiah." Ask baby James – he'll tell it all. I don't have to. I believe my son. He had no reason to lie. I told him, "it's okay; God will surely handle her for everything she did to y'all."

The system is a joke. Children will get removed from a home that's perfectly fine and be placed somewhere where things should never have been done. That's why out of all my kids, my two younger boys were the ones I worried and stressed about the most. It was like I felt what they were having to deal with. I had nothing but discomfort. I prayed the most for them. I knew in my heart that Pooter and Janay were okay.

My heart and soul really began to ease the moment I got the boys home. So did theirs – especially Messiah's. The worst part of his abuse was that he couldn't talk yet to tell anything. But if you knew my baby, the day I got him back, the expression on his face was enough for anyone to know something was wrong and had been for a while.

I don't blame their dad. Baby James always said that when things occurred, his dad was at work. One thing about karma: when it hits, there's no dodging it. It comes in different ways, forms, and fashions. All I can do is pray for that girl.

Every last one of my children suffered. The hardest part for me was not being there when they needed me the most, not the fact that they were gone. I knew they were coming back home. Not being able to comfort them in these situations that they should have never been in – that's what hurt me the most.

5

The intake worker had a serious personal vendetta against me. It became obvious when I received my discovery packet and attached were my personal Facebook posts. She had it out for me to the point she damn near became obsessively crazy with thinking as many things as she could to hurt me in some of the worst ways possible that came to her mind. This woman went on Facebook, typed in my name, and began searching for whatever she could about me. That was her doing; nobody told her to do that.

So yeah, it was plain to see right there that my situation was bigger than my children. When it became personal to her, all bets were off. If it were left to her, my children would have never come home. Already, using the little bit of power she had, she had started pursuing that, especially with James and Messiah 's dad, telling him that I wasn't allowed any kind of contact with my kids or she'd take them from him. She also told my children's father that he didn't need to deal with anyone but her. This was after I had been placed with a caseworker.

Eventually, when my children's father and I spoke again, this is what he told me. He also said that the reason he never brought the boys to the agency for visits with me is because she had told him he didn't have to. I had kind of figured myself that she was still contacting him, when she never was supposed to once her intake job was done. The next step is a caseworker gets assigned, and from then on, everything should be handled by that individual and no one else.

My caseworker kept saying to my kids' aunt, "I don't know who he's talking to. I haven't spoken with him at all. Every time I call I get his voicemail, so who's telling him the boys have a no-contact order with Darnice? That's a lie." It was the intake worker from hell.

6

I truly believe Pooter was a victim who was verbally abused and coerced into saying things that never came out of his mouth, set up by the school staff. How crazy does this sound? The school was called Mahoning County High, and the name of the jail in our city is Mahoning County Jail. My boy should have never been in that type of environment.

28

The judge who's over the school is the same one who runs our juvenile department.

The greatest evils in the world will not be carried out by men with guns but by men with suits sitting behind desks. I believe that judge might have even been the one giving orders that my children couldn't go to another school, even after pressing charges against me. I find it so ludicrous that when my children got back home with me, that's exactly where they stayed. I had to take my children out of the school district.

People with authority, which is power, abuse it. Human beings are so stupid. They take their authority and think it's limitless. That's why humans will never ever have it, because the key to power is to never lose it, and what do they do with authority? They abuse it until eventually it's gone.

So Davie had her issues; she had to fight alone. Pooter had his. James was watching his younger brother get abused, and Messiah was being abused. My children's strength is unbelievable. Take our story and know that we loved each other and weren't going to stop fighting until we were back together. We are all we have. There's no me without my children, and there's no them without me.

I started my foundation from love. One of the things God was trying to tell me was to get them out of that school. Our trials and tribulations were not only a testament meant to be told but now a story to be heard. God says if we come to him, he'll give us peace, but in the world we'll have trials of various kinds. But he has overcome the world. As I grew closer to the Lord during this time, it really changed me in a great way. I appreciate our storm; I gained a lot from it.

God gave me patience throughout this horrifying situation. I had no choice but to use it. Literally everything was out of my control, but I constantly prayed. Prayer really became more consistent with me and in my life, more than ever before. It was a morning routine, afternoon, evening, and all throughout the day. It was all one deep prayer for everyone. I believed in Jesus, and I patiently knew he had heard every cry and felt every teardrop.

Eventually, I could feel the uplifting of every demon that was trying to attack me. It was God and his mercy that kept my sanity. Prayer changes things. I'll tell anybody. I'll shout and praise God forevermore. God has been so good to me.

At one point, I started to become anxious and unable to sleep because I was gratefully thanking God for how he had delivered me. It was unexplainably heartwarming. Can you imagine not being able to sleep because of God's mercifulness? He laid upon me all the blessings of the spirit. He had been with me throughout my entire situation. At times, I thought I wasn't going survive, but the God we serve is unbelievably amazing.

7

I love the good book. It will be forever my all-time favorite. I love a wise person. I love listening to anyone who has experienced life and can share it. People like that are God-sent.

One who I had in my life was Mama. As I was growing up from a child to a teenager and then an adult, she taught me so many things. My grandmother was an amazingly wise woman. I still remember every talk and all the conversations we shared about different life situations and experiences, good and bad. So of course, I now pass that wisdom on to my daughter, and when my sons come of age, I'll pass it on to them as well.

You see, when you ask God for changes through prayer, you change as well. It gives you a better outlook on life. You begin to appreciate what you have a little more – at least you should. I sure did. My family was dismantled and torn up for a great while, but when God restored us, I valued my children in a way I never had before.

God tells us to ask him for whatever it is our heart desires, and we'll receive it. He tells us he'll never leave us or forsake us. God says he'll never put more on us than we can bear. I've experienced it all in this situation; that's why my faith is the way it is.

My name and my face have been dragged through the media – newspapers and even radio – by gossiping people. I still could not care less what anyone thinks of me. I know what kind of person I am. If I lived to care about what opinions get formed of me, I would have died years ago. The four little ones I have are the only opinions that will ever matter to me.

The things life hits us with are not always favorable, but we pray. What an everlasting flow of righteousness! I love the faith that God has set upon my soul. It is such an awesome feeling of relief. The storm, our storm, that separated me from my children allowed me to open up so much that giving my heartaches and pain to God was the only thing I knew to do. Without God, there was no way possible. God does the impossible.

I surrendered everything I had bottled up inside. It was enough to have driven a sane person to a mental institution. I amazed myself with the will, the strength, and the determination to fight the devils and demons that were attacking me and my babies. It was truly an ongoing hell. But look at me – I'm here, I survived, and I'm sharing my story with the world, letting them know what God can and will do.

This is my testimony. I now think like this: God chose my family. He chose us for a reason. It was not until this horrifying experience that, slowly but surely, I began to see what God was trying to tell me and wanted to give me. All I wanted was my children. Nothing or nobody else mattered. In my absence, I just wanted them nurtured, safe, and sound.

The Messiah between me and my children is unbreakable. Demons and devils tried throwing fireballs. Each attack was stronger and heavier than the one before. That only made me stronger, though I felt weaker than I ever had in my entire life. I wanted to commit suicide. Yes, this horrifying trial that separated me from my children had me feeling suicidal for the first time in my life. It was my breaking point.

8

Never in my life have I seen so many people with evil intentions and devilish ways. My heart was broken in ways you can't begin to imagine. But my soul was on fire. My faith was tested so many times, but as weak as I felt, God maximized my strength to endure everything. I felt like I was carrying the weight of a mountain on my shoulders. I felt like a walking zombie in a tunnel of everlasting terror.

My children – Janay, Pooter, James, and Messiah – were the reasons I was fighting for my family. Life had no meaning to me without them. They were my life, because they gave me life. So yeah, I definitely felt like life had been taken from me.

As days, weeks, and months passed, I finally got my life somewhat in order. I also realized that obedience is something else God was teaching me. Pay attention to things God is trying to tell you, because ignoring him can cause unimaginable pain. Writing became so therapeutic to me that it began to give me peace of mind.

Look how much God loved me. He came right on in at the perfect time to save my heart and soul. He gave me writing to soothe the pain my soul was feeling. He brought love back into my heart by doing so. Love was something I had lost, hopelessly, when they took my children away from me. By writing, I had the ability to release everything from my mind when I had nobody or no energy to talk to anyone else. It was just me and my thoughts.

The only thing I can do now is continue to learn how to correct mistakes. How can you learn from mistakes if you don't make any? That's where failure practices come in. I tell myself this all the time in life: when you have the opportunity to do right, do it. Those things you can't go back and change are now lessons learned.

9

Although I had the intake lady from hell, my initial caseworker was awesome. So was her supervisor. My child services worker was actually on my side; she had my back. So that was a blessing. She helped me in as many ways as possible.

My attorney was also great. Of the many court-appointed attorneys, he was one who actually worked for me and not for the system. He was the attorney I had for my child services case. He gave me guidance on getting my children home as quickly as possible.

I moved to Cleveland, Ohio, in June of 2019. I called my parole officer to let her know. She said that I couldn't just up and do that, but I expressed to her that it would be better for my children and me. She said, "well, Darnice, I don't want to hold you back. Let me talk to the judge to see what I can do."

God is just amazing, and there you have it. In July of 2019, after only having to be on adult parole for five months, I was released.

While the weekend order was in place, Pooter, who was also playing football, wanted to continue. So even having him living in Cleveland stopped nothing. I set up arrangements for someone to bring him down to Youngstown. For over a year, I paid someone who agreed upon sixty dollars a week to transport him back and forth. I was just thankful to get my baby home. He played football the entire season. He didn't miss one game.

I tried to make sure Pooter knew and understood that I loved him, and that he was going to come back home. I tried to make sure I took care of him and his necessities before the other children, because the other children had something Pooter didn't: me. I felt so much pain inside my heart because of it. When would it be over? How much more pain would my family have to continue to go through over a blown-out-of-proportion lie?

From the beginning, the staff at Mahoning County High called Pooter to the office and yelled at him. This was the child services officer who talked him into making a statement that he got a whopping when he was bad at school. That's what Pooter told them.

I said, "son, I'm not mad because you said that. I'll tell them too." But all the other bull crap that led to them taking my children was false. It turned into an accusation that Pooter was being beaten by Brian, my boyfriend, which never came out of Pooter's mouth.

It was ugly from start to finish. None of it made any sense to me. From the beginning, three of my children were back home living with me. They were only gone for two months, but it took Pooter over a year to come home. What was different about the others? I found it crazy that nobody could make sense of it rationally.

This nightmare became seemingly a joke to someone. They didn't even have an existing court date for me to get Pooter back. I called my attorney, and he filed for one. I started to take action in any way I could. If I hadn't thought to do so, it would have only added an extended time before my son could come home.

This intake person had Pooter going through pure hell. She had Janay wanting to be home so bad, she even asked for the woman's number herself. She said, "no, Mommy, I want to come home. I don't want to live like this."

James and Messiah had to deal with verbal, mental, and physical abuse. The worst part was that my two-year-old, Messiah, couldn't even talk to tell anyone. But baby James could.

My kids each, individually, were left alone to deal with issues no children should have to by themselves. The situation was out of my control. This right here is the very reason it still hurts today. I was hurt badly when they were taken from me, but I knew God was going to bring my babies back home.

It hurt the worst when they needed me in their lives the most and I couldn't be there for them. Again, their ages were two, six, eleven, and thirteen. They had to fight these battles on their own, and this should have never happened to them or to me.

10

On October 22, 2018, I went to court. Custody had been granted back to me for Pooter. Prior to that, he was only allowed to come home on weekends. It had been a year, one week, and four days since he was taken from me. I cried and said, "thank you, God!"

No children were allowed in the courtroom. Pooter stayed in the hallway and was determined to find the judge. I said "there she is" to Pooter, because he had asked for her. He followed her outside the building. I said, "what did you say to her?"

He said he told her, "thank you for letting me go back home to my mom."

On February 7, 2019, I went to court regarding my criminal case. After numerous court hearings, my criminal case was finally settled. My original charge, which was a felony, involved inducing panic and carried a three-year prison term. It was reduced by my lawyer to a nonviolent crime, which was obstructing official business. It was still a felony, though, because the crime was assault with intent. The felony just became a lesser one, with me being on adult parole authority for a year. The judge also said that because I had gone all my life without any record, after my year of parole was up, he would expunge my record. He emphasized that he understood being a parent is not an easy job.

March 20, 2019, marked the end of my case with Children Services. Thank you, God. It was all over, finally. I know many people found great humor in my horrible nightmare. I don't care. Laugh on – the joke's on you. The gracious God I serve is always thinking ahead. God has always replaced anything I've ever lost. For every moment we suffered through our storm, he is going to give us ten times that in luxurious days. If our storm didn't exist, I wouldn't have a story to tell. I may have lifted up someone's spirits and given a weak person strength.

At your weakest moments, that's what God will do: give you strength. I healed a broken heart. I made a disbeliever believe. I made someone cry. I made somebody believe in the power of prayer. I may have even restored someone's faith. To the people who love me, this situation probably angered you, as it once did me. But it's over now, and it allowed me to do what I always do: help somebody.

To me, what you go through and get through in life is what develops you. Our storm, which had an ugly beginning, ended graciously. I developed my passion for writing during adversity. I've always wanted to open up a business, and now look at what God has done. He gave me a different calling, which was part of his plan from the beginning.

This warms my heart. My family was chosen. I have been chosen. I have been writing this book for over a year, and because I put so much of my time and energy into writing out a part of my life, now you have it, my business: my first book.

Here are a few Bible verses that have helped me along the way. I hope many will find these useful as well:

- I have said these things to you, that in me you may have peace. In the world you will have tribulation. But take heart; I have overcome the world. ~John 16:33
- Count it all joy, my brothers, when you have trials of various kinds. ~James 1:2
- And after you have suffered a little while, the God of all grace, who has called you to his eternal glory in Christ, will himself restore, confirm, strengthen and establish you. ~1 Peter 5:10
- And the peace of God, which surpasses all understanding, will guard your hearts and your minds in Christ Jesus. ~Philippians 4:7
- For we walk by faith, not by sight. ~2 Corinthians 5:7
- Blessed is the man who remains steadfast under trial; for when he has stood the test he will receive the crown of life, which God has promised to those who love him. ~James 1:12
- When the righteous cry out for help, the Lord hears and delivers them out of all their troubles. The Lord is near to the brokenhearted and saves the crushed in spirit. ~Psalm 34:17-18
- Trust in the Lord with all your heart, and do not lean on your own understanding. In all ways acknowledge him, and he will make straight your paths. ~Proverbs 3:5-6
- Therefore do not throw away your confidence, which has a great reward. ~Hebrews 10:35

I've listed characteristics of my children for everyone to get a brief insight. These are the qualities that define them, part of the human nature that God gave them.

Janay, my daughter, my eldest child, takes charge in any situation. She has my back, front, right, and left. She takes good care of her brothers, protecting them with everything in her. She's very smart and intelligent. She catches on to things quickly – such a fast learner. I love it. Always, since she was a baby, she could tell easily when an adult was pulling bull crap.

Jondell (Pooter), my second born, my eldest son, makes an impression on whoever he meets. He is an unforgettable kid who will do everything in his being for his mother to lack nothing, no matter the circumstances. He has always been this way. This is one kid of mine who'll take care of me when I'm old and gray – my little provider, destined for greatness since he was in the womb.

James, my second son, tells me he loves me every day, about a hundred times a day. I love it. This boy of mine will go to war with anybody when it comes to me, and it has always been this way. My little protector – he has so much courage and heart, he almost fears nothing. My left-handed child has great comprehension and thinks of things average kids his age wouldn't. He's really gifted and will definitely keep you laughing. He is such a joy to have around.

Messiah, my baby boy, smiles all the time. He is so full of life and energy. He has such a happy soul.

I thank God for all four of my children. People define riches and wealth differently, and you all are mine. Thank you for being who you are, special in your own way. The Messiah I share with each of you is simply amazing. Love, Mommy.

I'd like to dedicate my first book to a few of my family members: my mother and father, my grandmother we called Mama; my grandmother Shuler; my daughter, Asani; and David.

ACKNOWLEDGMENTS

I would like to give all the glory to the higher power, my children, and my siblings.

A MESSAGE TO MY OFFSPRING

With great heart comes great sacrifice, and great determination doesn't come with you because it lives in you. Don't ever stop; don't ever settle. Recondition your minds as if what you're aiming for doesn't exist.

Love,
Mommy